Lenten Days
Lenten Grace

Lenten Days
Lenten Grace

forty days with Jesus

By
Raymond Chapman

Pauline
BOOKS & MEDIA
Boston

Library of Congress Cataloging-in-Publication Data

Chapman, Raymond.
  Lenten days, Lenten grace : forty days with Jesus / Raymond
Chapman.
    p. cm.
Originally published: Norwich, Norfolk : Canterbury Press, 1999.
  ISBN 0-8198-4491-8 (pbk.)
  Lent—Prayer-books and devotions—English. I. Title.
  BV85 .C47 2001
  242'.34—dc21

                                        2001003902

Chapman, Raymond. Originally published in England under the title
Days of Grace by the Canterbury Press Norwich of St Mary's Works,
St Mary's Plain, Norwich, Norfolk, NR3 3BH UK.

The Scripture quotations contained herein are from the *New Revised
Standard Version Bible. Catholic Edition,* copyright © 1993 and 1989
by the Division of Christian Education of the National Council of the
Churches of Christ in the U.S.A. Used by permission. All rights re-
served.

In extracts from other sources the language and usage of the original
have been preserved.

Printed and published in 2002 in the U.S.A. by Pauline Books &
Media, 50 Saint Pauls Avenue, Boston, MA 02130-3491.

www.pauline.org

Pauline Books & Media is the publishing house of the Daughters of
St. Paul, an international congregation of women religious serving
the Church with the communications media.

1 2 3 4 5 6 7 8 9   07 06 05 04 03 02 01

Contents

Introduction

The traditional practice of keeping a period of forty days before Easter as a time of fasting and penance has made many people associate Lent mainly with self-denial or "giving up something." To abstain can be a valuable means of discipline and of strengthening ourselves as we live the Christian way. It is not, however, the whole purpose of Lent and should accompany the more important resolution to spend more time in prayer and reflection, both private and liturgical. Lent is a time to consider God's love and our sins, to repent and seek to do better. It is a time to reflect on our spiritual state and our response to God's immense love for each one of us.

The reflections which follow are proposed for each day of Lent, excluding Sundays (which are not counted within the forty days). For the first four days of Lent, we prepare by reflecting on our human condition with its failures and its hopes. Each of Lent's five weeks is centered on a theme which is prominent in Scripture and can focus our thoughts and prayers, giving us images to bring to our own situations. Over five weeks, we consider Jour-

neys, Mountains, Light, Nourishment, and Healing. Each
of these helps us to think about our faith-life as we journey through our days. In Holy Week the five themes bring
us to a contemplation of the Paschal Mystery.

The reflections for each day follow a pattern:

A passage from Scripture, sometimes abridged from
the full account, to give the central message. Having these
short passages within this book may be helpful for those
of us "on the go."

A commentary to give some background and suggest
ideas arising from the passage.

A meditation, using the passage imaginatively to con-
nect it with our own experiences and to help us respond
to what it might be saying to us.

Questions for reflection to make our meditation as
concrete as possible.

An invitation to praise, and prayer to help in form-
ing a practical resolution from the meditation.

A short phrase to be repeated during the day, which
will frequently return our mind to what has been learned.

It would be ideal to designate a certain time, as early
as possible in the day, for additional daily reflection during Lent. But we should not be discouraged if our busy
lives demand a more flexible approach. Anxiety and haste
are useless, and it is better to pray for a shorter time with

full attention than to be going through the motions with an eye on the clock.

Lent is a solemn time, but it is not meant to be a miserable one. Sorrow for our sins and for the suffering of our Lord are, in God's mercy, a means of growth in a more joyful and richer life of faith. We may want to keep before us one of the most comforting and encouraging sayings of Jesus: "I came that they may have life, and have it more abundantly" (Jn 10:10).

PREPARATION DAYS

In these first four days, our reflections prepare us for the explorations that we will make into some images of God's revelation. We consider who we are and our identity as members of the human race which God created to live in this world. We recognize that we have all, individually and collectively, fallen away from the loving obedience that God desires for us. We think of the paschal mystery, which restored us and which is the focus of our Lenten meditations. We try to discern God's will for us and pray to be guided in all that we experience this Lent.

Ash Wednesday

Who are we?

Genesis 1:26–28, 31

Then God said, "Let us make humankind in our image, according to our likeness; and let them have dominion over the fish of the sea, and over the birds of the air, and over the cattle, and over all the wild animals of the earth, and over every creeping thing that creeps upon the earth." So God created humankind in his image, in the image of God he created them; male and female he created them. God blessed them, and.... God saw everything that he had made, and indeed, it was very good.

What God made was good. How could it be otherwise, since its source was infinite goodness and love? At this time above all others in the year, we acknowledge our sins and respond in repentance. We cannot understand the horror of sin unless we see it as an offense against God, who made all things good. We were made in the Divine image not by some distant, all-powerful being, but by One who made us to share perfection. By making "lenten resolutions," we are not trying to placate an angry God but to come back to the loving God who is reaching out and calling us to become what we were created to be.

––––––––––

Rest in silence and feel the love of God who made you part of a magnificent creation. Think of something that gives you great delight and a sense of God's presence: a scene of natural beauty, a painting, a piece of music, or someone you really love.

God loves you with an intensity far greater than any delight you can feel in this world. God loves you as you are, knowing the depths of your being, and offers you this love to restore the divine image in you. See this Lent as a way of returning to God. Picture yourself among a great multitude of Christians who are on their way back to original holiness.

Am I convinced of God's passionate love for me? Do I respond in obedience to the divine will, not as a constraint on my personal freedom but as a fulfillment of my true self?

Spend some time thanking God for life and for the loving care you've received up to this day. Rejoice that you are inspired to come to God in trust this Lent.

———————

Almighty Father, Creator and sustainer of
all, guide us toward yourself during this season
and give us grace to keep what we resolve.
May we always remember your loving purpose
that made all things good and honor your
divine image in ourselves and in all people.

**God saw all of creation,
and it was very good.**

Thursday

What have we become?

Genesis 2:16–17; 3:4–6, 23–24

The Lord God commanded the man, "You may freely eat of every tree of the garden; but of the tree of the knowledge of good and evil you shall not eat, for in the day that you eat of it you shall die." But the serpent said to the woman, "You will not die, for God knows that when you eat of it your eyes will be opened, and you will be like God, knowing good and evil." So when the woman saw that the tree was good for food, and that it was a delight to the eyes, and that the tree was to be desired to make one wise, she took of its fruit and ate; and she also gave some to her husband, who was with her, and he ate. Therefore the Lord God sent him forth from the garden of Eden, to till the ground from which he was taken. He drove out the man; and at the east of the garden of Eden he placed the cherubim, and a sword flaming and turning to guard the way to the tree of life.

The story of Adam and Eve eating the forbidden fruit and leaving the Garden of Eden is familiar even to people who know very little of the Bible. It is a way of expressing that human beings, made in the image of God, disobeyed. They misused the gift of free choice which God had given them. Those made to be most like God, made to live happily and to care for the created world, were the very ones who rebelled. This is "original sin," which is not just the action of some distant ancestor but which, in some way, makes it easier for us to turn away from God and follow our own ways.

————

Think of the sorrow you have felt after hurting someone you really love, and how much you desired to "make it up" to them. Even more should we desire to turn from our sins and accept God's great love for us.

What is my first reaction when I realize I have failed? How does fear that my good image has been compromised figure into my sorrow for sin?

Be thankful that sorrow for sin is the beginning of deep conversion. Give praise for your desire to have a closer relationship with God.

————

Loving Father, grant that during this Lent we will find a spirit of true repentance, a desire to do better, and the grace to live according to your Word of life.

**I acknowledge my faults
and never forget my sin.**

Friday

What has God done for us?

Romans 5:12, 15–17

Sin came into the world through one man, and death came through sin, and so death spread to all because all have sinned. But the free gift was not like the trespass. For if the many died through the one man's trespass, much more surely have the grace of God and the free gift...of the one man, Jesus Christ, abounded for the many. And the free gift is not like the effect of the one man's sin. For the judgment following one trespass brought condemnation, but the free gift following many trespasses brings justification. If, because of the one man's trespass, death exercised dominion through that one, much more surely will those who receive the abundance of grace and the free gift of righteousness exercise dominion in life through the one man, Jesus Christ.

Here is the amazing truth of the Christian mystery: we have been restored by the human obedience of God. We are forgiven not by our own efforts, but by love freely given to those who have chosen things other than God. This new creation is even more wonderful than the first, because God has now shared our human condition, with all its joys and sorrows, its ups and downs. What a gift this is for us!

––––––

Quiet yourself and picture something meaningful to you which represents a change from trouble to relief, from sadness to joy. It may be light coming from darkness; release from a locked room; receiving back something precious that has been lost; love restored after estrangement; health after sickness. Recall during this Lent that you are acceptable because God has received you back and made you whole.

What "locked room" might I need to have opened by the healing, "wholing" power of God? Is there room in my life for trust?

Thank God for new life in Christ — life that springs from love.

––––––

Blessed Christ, whose love has gifted us with life, be our example, our guide and our strength throughout this Lent and for all our lives.

**Christ died
so that I might live.**

Saturday

What does God want us to do?

John 15:12–17

"This is my commandment, that you love one another as I have loved you. No one has greater love than this, to lay down one's life for one's friends. You are my friends if you do what I command you. I do not call you servants any longer, because the servant does not know what the master is doing; but I have called you friends, because I have made known to you everything that I have heard from my Father. You did not choose me but I chose you. And I appointed you to go and bear fruit, fruit that will last, so that the Father will give you whatever you ask him in my name. I am giving you these commands so that you may love one another."

The Prophet Micah describes a life of discipleship: "What does the Lord require of you but to do justice, and to love kindness, and to walk humbly with your God?" (6:8) We can live as disciples because we are empowered by the Holy Spirit which Christ promised to his disciples. Through Christ's death, we have a new freedom, not to live selfishly following our worst inclinations, but to live as we were meant to live, as images of God restored. We are called to obey the commands of our Lord, and to show our love of God by our love for others. The Greek text in this passage uses the word *agape:* the same that St. Paul uses in his great hymn to love (1 Cor 13). It is a love that is absolute, not responding to the worthiness of its object, but seeking to imitate the unbounded love of God.

―――――

Quietly imagine yourself among the disciples on the eve of Jesus' death. Your beloved Master has said that he is going away. You hear his words of comfort and instruction, and think that they may be the last teaching you will have from him. How eagerly you would listen and resolve to obey! Move into the coming weeks in that strength.

What passage of Scripture speaks most reassuringly to me about God's love for me? Is there a way that I can make God's Word a more influential part of my daily life?

Remain quiet for a moment. Thank God for speaking to you during your lenten moments of prayer. Be joyful in your heart, even as you recognize your sins and reflect on the sufferings of our Lord.

———————

Lord our God, be with us during these lenten days. Walk with us, illumine our path, and let us feel your nearness.

**Love one another,
as I have loved you.**

WEEK 1: JOURNEYS

The Bible is full of movement: journeys of a few hours or of many years; journeys taken at the command of God; journeys to escape from danger; journeys to begin a new phase of life. The image of human life as a journey from birth to death is strong and meaningful. Like travelers on the road, we meet new people, see new places, and move toward our destination. Sometimes the road is smooth and easy, sometimes we labor to gain a short distance. At certain times we seem to remain for long in the same place, and at other times we move quickly.

As we make our journey this Lent, we can look at a few Scripture stories and relate them to our own way forward. Are we growing in our life of love, or have we stopped too long at a comfortable place and feel no inclination to move on?

Week 1: Monday

Journey into the Unknown

Genesis 12:1–4

Now the LORD said to Abram, "Go from your country and your kindred and your father's house to the land that I will show you. I will make of you a great nation, and I will bless you, and make your name great, so that you will be a blessing. I will bless those who bless you, and the one who curses you I will curse; and in you all the families of the earth shall be blessed." So Abram went, as the LORD had told him; and Lot went with him. Abram was seventy-five years old when he departed from Haran.

Abram is the first to be told of God's special purpose for humanity. He is the supreme patriarch, from whom would come the Chosen People of Israel. The beginning of his story involves a call to leave his native place for an unknown land to which God will lead him. His immediate obedience required great faith and courage, not only to leave all that he knew but to take his family into the many perils of travel in the ancient world.

Today we seldom start on a journey without knowing our destination, but every day we are continuing the journey of life without certain knowledge of the future. Scripture reminds us, "Do not boast about tomorrow, for you do not know what a day may bring" (Prov 27:1). If we seek God's guidance, we shall go on our way with confidence, sure that our direction is right even though the next stage is not yet revealed.

———————

Step out into Lent with the trust that Abram showed when he walked away from Haran to follow God's calling. Try to imagine how he felt when, already an old man, he was told to leave everything and begin a journey to a strange land. Think about the faith which made him sure that God would fulfill the promise, the faith that sustained him through many years of journeying and perplexity. Be open to God's guidance, not seeking after certainty but trusting that God's purposes are good.

What keeps me from completely surrendering to God in trust? Is there a way I might be able to make a small step toward trusting God in some area of my life?

Thank God for giving you the desire to entrust your ways to the Lord.

———————

Lord Jesus, may you be our companion and our guide, through this season and through all our lives. May we follow your example, and may we find in you assurance that wherever we find ourselves, you are with us.

**Praise God for the past;
trust God for the future.**

Week 1: Tuesday

Journey into the Wilderness

Exodus 6:2, 6–8

God spoke to Moses and said to him: "Say therefore to the Israelites, 'I am the LORD, and I will free you from the burdens of the Egyptians and deliver you from slavery to them. I will redeem you with an outstretched arm and with mighty acts of judgment. I will take you as my people, and I will be your God. You shall know that I am the LORD your God, who has freed you from the burdens of the Egyptians. I will bring you into the land that I swore to give to Abraham, Isaac, and Jacob; I will give it to you for a possession. I am the LORD.'"

The Exodus from Egypt was remembered by Israel as the greatest sign of God's care for the chosen people. God led them through the wilderness for forty years, going before them under the sign of cloud by day and fire by night. Their journey began with a miraculous crossing of the Red Sea and ended with crossing the River Jordan into the Promised Land. It was during the wilderness journey that they received the Law through Moses, overcame many enemies, and experienced God's loving care many times. Yet they often grumbled and longed for the familiar daily routine of the slavery from which they had been freed. In later years, the prophets sometimes admonished the Israelites for becoming soft and complacent in their settled life, and contrasted it with what, by that time, seemed the purity of the wilderness.

––––––

Think of the children of Israel going out in families, with all the possessions they could carry, into a strange, perilous world. Imagine the vast emptiness, the pitiless sun by day and the cold, unprotected desert by night. They learned to depend on God alone for their survival.

Consider how you depend on God for your very existence, for loving support until this moment and for everything in your future. In the silence of prayer, be alone with God in the needy, desert places of your soul, and feel the love that fills what seems to be emptiness.

When my journey towards God leads me into strange places, how do I hold fast in trust that I am guided? When days are long and weary, how can I still give praise for all that God is for me?

Give thanks for all of God's blessings on your journey through life.

Lord of the wilderness, be close to us in dry
and barren times, and keep us faithful in times
of peace. Let us never trust in our own strength,
but rejoice in the love that keeps our feet from
wandering and that will bring us to the
promised land of eternal life.

**Lead me on, Lord,
by day and night,
until the journey ends.**

Week 1: Wednesday

Journey of Disobedience

Jonah 1:1–4, 7, 12, 15, 17

The word of the LORD came to Jonah son of Amittai, saying, "Go at once to Nineveh, that great city, and cry out against it; for their wickedness has come up before me." But Jonah set out to flee to Tarshish from the presence of the LORD. He went down to Joppa and found a ship going to Tarshish.... But the LORD hurled a great wind upon the sea, and such a mighty storm came upon the sea that the ship threatened to break up. The sailors said to one another, "Come, let us cast lots, so that we may know on whose account this calamity has come upon us." So they cast lots, and the lot fell on Jonah. He said to them, "Pick me up and throw me into the sea; then the sea will quiet down for you; for I know it is because of me that this great storm has come upon you." So they picked Jonah up and threw him into the sea; and the sea ceased from its raging. But the LORD provided a large fish to swallow up Jonah; and Jonah was in the belly of the fish for three days and three nights.

Everyone knows the story of Jonah and the whale. For most people, the story ends with Jonah being cast safely upon dry land. In fact, the main point comes after this scene, when he succeeds in calling the people of Nineveh to repent and then sulks because God has spared them. Jonah has to learn that God's love is for all and God's pardon is unconditional for those who return in repentance.

To avoid an unwelcome duty to which God called him, Jonah sailed in an opposite direction and settled down to sleep while others were in danger. After a terrifying experience, he found himself where he should have gone in the first place. Jonah acted selfishly, but God remained faithful to the end.

———

Think of something you know you should do but that you continually avoid. (This exercise of the imagination will probably be an easy one!) It may be something simple: to visit someone in need whom you find boring, to write a helpful letter, or to be more committed to prayer. You have promised to follow Christ on your journey through life, but what happens when the going becomes difficult?

Like the shock of plunging into cold water, feel God's call, rousing you from your selfishness to a renewed choice for the good.

Can I name something good that I continually avoid doing because it is difficult? What would need to happen for me to have a change of heart in this area?

Thank God for the shocks and surprises of life that recall us to doing good. Praise God's loving call that is stronger than our selfish resistance.

———

Loving Father, calling us to conversion and using even our weak and selfish moments to proclaim the Good News, forgive our unwillingness to serve and make us instruments of your peace.

**Lord, keep me always
in the right way.**

Week 1: Thursday

Journey Day by Day

Matthew 2:1–5, 8–9, 11

In the time of King Herod, after Jesus was born in Bethlehem of Judea, wise men from the East came to Jerusalem, asking, "Where is the child who has been born king of the Jews? For we have observed his star at its rising, and have come to pay him homage." When King Herod heard this, he was frightened, and all Jerusalem with him; and calling together all the chief priests and scribes of the people, he inquired of them where the Messiah was to be born. They told him, "In Bethlehem of Judea." Then he sent them to Bethlehem, saying, "Go and search diligently for the child; and when you have found him, bring me word so that I may also go and pay him homage." When they had heard the king, they set out; and there, ahead of them, went the star that they had seen at its rising, until it stopped over the place where the child was. On entering the house, they saw the child with Mary his mother;

and they knelt down and paid him homage. Then, opening their treasure chests, they offered him gifts of gold, frankincense, and myrrh.

"A cold coming we had of it," T. S. Eliot wrote of the journey of the Magi. They traveled day by day, without fully understanding their purpose, knowing only that they were being led by a star of unusual significance. They may have wondered why they, Gentiles from another land, were called to worship the King of the Jews. When they came to Herod, who claimed that title, they knew that this was not the end of their quest and went on until they found a newborn baby. They knelt and worshiped him.

We know this pasage well, but we hear only the end of the story and perhaps do not reflect on the long journey which the magi had taken in faith: a faith not yet understood, but used by God to bring them into his incarnate presence and to be a sign that salvation was for everyone.

————————

Quietly imagine yourself on a long journey, far from home and uncertain of your destination. Every night you have to seek shelter in a strange place, among people of a different language and culture. It is cold at night; sometimes a place to rest is hard to find, and sleep, when it finally comes, is imperfect. After a few hours you must start again on the weary way, knowing only that there is a sign that must be followed to the journey's end.

In what ways do I demand certainty and clarity regarding God's desires for my life? What might keep me journeying on toward God without continually reaching after certainty?

Thank God for the faith that is sufficient for each day. Give praise for the guidance of Scripture and the gift of prayer.

———————

Alone with none but you, our God,
  We journey on our way.
  What need we fear when you are near,
  O King of night and day?
  More safe we are within your hand
  Than if a host did 'round us stand.

St. Columba

Christ, be my guiding star today.

Week 1: Friday

Journey in Fear

Matthew 2:13–15

An angel of the Lord appeared to Joseph in a dream and said, "Get up, take the child and his mother, and flee to Egypt, and remain there until I tell you; for Herod is about to search for the child, to destroy him." Then Joseph got up, took the child and his mother by night, and went to Egypt, and remained there until the death of Herod.

Although the Magi traveled with hardship, they hoped for an end that would crown their journey. Instead, the Holy Family went away by night, driven by the warning of danger to the beloved baby of whom so much had been promised.

The command to go into Egypt would make the journey seem even more threatening, for Egypt was the land of former slavery, the land from which Israel had been delivered and brought to freedom. It could have seemed as if all were being reversed, as if God's promises were being revoked and the one who had been promised as the Savior had to return to the place of captivity. But God's great purpose would again be revealed: this was a symbolic repeating of the first deliverance, leading to a greater one. For Jesus, it was the first of many journeys and wanderings that would follow in the years of his ministry, until his final journey to Jerusalem and the Cross.

———————

Quietly imagine the fear of that first night of escape, felt by millions of people in the years that have followed this Gospel event. Can you begin to imagine the sufferings of refugees driven from their homes by war, persecution, famine? Picture travelers with no destination, with no thought except the drive to move on. Let your heart go out to them. It is too much to grasp fully, but try to open yourself to God's love for all who suffer.

As you live this lenten season, make sure that your focus does not become self-centered. Let your meditation strengthen your compassion and intercession for others. When you feel yourself drawn from your safe, familiar ways, pray that your trust in God will be strengthened. Every journey has a beginning and an end, and even if the beginning brings doubt and fear, the end can lead to a new revelation of God's purpose.

When problems seem too great or a situation too threatening, how might I remind myself of the loving presence of God even then? Is there something I can do to help someone in need today?

Thank God for all the guidance you have received and not recognized at the time. Give praise for joy that perhaps began in anxiety.

———————

Gracious Lord, keep us strong in faith and hope when we feel doubtful. Bless us when we are anxious and uncertain about the future, and keep us close to you. Have mercy on all who wander with no resting place, and all whose minds are restless because they do not know the love that is in Christ.

**There is no fear
when God is leading.**

Week 1: Saturday

Journey for the Gospel

Acts 14:1–2, 5–7, 19–20

In Iconium Paul and Barnabas went into the Jewish synagogue and spoke in such a way that a great number of both Jews and Greeks became believers. But the unbelieving Jews stirred up the Gentiles and poisoned their minds against the brothers. And when an attempt was made by both Gentiles and Jews, with their rulers, to mistreat them and to stone them, the apostles learned of it and fled to Lystra and Derbe, cities of Lycaonia, and to the surrounding country; and there they continued proclaiming the good news. But Jews came there from Antioch and Iconium and won over the crowds. Then they stoned Paul and dragged him out of the city, supposing that he was dead. But when the disciples surrounded him, he got up and went into the city. The next day he went on with Barnabas to Derbe.

Paul and Barnabas were following the command Jesus gave at his Ascension, to bring the message of salvation to the whole world. St. Paul was the first to teach that the New Covenant was for everyone who would receive it. He made many journeys, suffered much, and eventually died as a martyr.

The Church has grown through the work of missionaries and teachers, often in danger and privation. God's messengers have always journeyed into the unknown, some by going to distant lands and some while remaining at home. These have been journeys taken in faith, without looking for reward. If you read this entire chapter in Acts, you see how the people of Lystra first worshiped Paul and Barnabas as gods and then turned against them. On our journey through life, when we meet disappointments and feel let down, we remember that we are sharing the experience of so many who have gone before us in faith.

———

Imagine yourself setting out on a journey to a place where the people have never heard of Jesus Christ. They may be indifferent, mocking, hostile, or violent. What would you say to them? Would your actions show the love that was in your heart? Imagine you are quite alone, without the support of family, friends, or church. Only God is with you as you are sent to do this work.

Think of these things and then consider the opportunities that are available to you, the people you may be able to bring to Christ by pointing out his love for them in their situations. Your personal missionary journey may not be as demanding as Paul's, but there is still work to be done.

How do my faith and my way of life reinforce each other? How is God's love evident in my relationships?

Thank God for all the people who have led you to faith and helped you on your spiritual journey. Give praise for the freedom that the Gospel brings. Pray for missionaries and evangelists.

———————

Lord, as we travel through this season, grant us the faith that has given strength to those who have gone before us on the journey, and grace to follow their good example in showing that faith through word and deed until the journey ends.

**Lord, take my lips
and speak through them.**

WEEK 2: MOUNTAINS

Not many of us have attempted the great mountain-climbing feats that attract public attention, but perhaps we know what it's like to climb a small hill and stand on its summit. From the summit, we behold a new view of the surrounding countryside, laid out and extending far beyond what we can see when we stand at its own level. We behold a new vision: details which previously seemed to be separate are now seen as part of a wider pattern. Although we do not think that heaven is "up there," somewhere in the sky, we do feel lifted up from the earth, closer to God in the stillness.

It is on the mountaintop that God is often revealed to people in Scripture. As we meditate on some of these "mountain experiences," we can relate them to our own lives. These are moments on the journey when we take time to go apart, to renew our commitment and to assess our spiritual living more deeply than we may do in our daily lives.

Week 2: Monday

Mountain of the Law

Exodus 24:12, 15–18

The LORD said to Moses, "Come up to me on the mountain, and wait there; and I will give you the tablets of stone, with the law and the commandment, which I have written for their instruction." Then Moses went up on the mountain, and the cloud covered the mountain. The glory of the LORD settled on Mount Sinai, and the cloud covered it for six days; on the seventh day he called to Moses out of the cloud. Now the appearance of the glory of the LORD was like a devouring fire on the top of the mountain in the sight of the people of Israel. Moses entered the cloud, and went up on the mountain. Moses was on the mountain for forty days and forty nights.

Mount Sinai was the mountain of the Law, where God entrusted Moses with the commandments on which Israel's religion would rest. God's Law stands firm forever and cannot be changed by our preference or destroyed by our rejection.

Through grace in Christ, we are forgiven when we repent and want to be reconciled for a fresh start. We have been freed from the fear of a judgment that will accept no defense and from the despair of knowing that we continually fail even when we most desire to live closely to God. Let us never allow our freedom in Christ to become an excuse for indifference. A life that follows selfish desires, not seeking to follow God's will, is not the Christian life.

———————

Have you ever been in a solitary place and felt the wonder and majesty of God? Even a brief escape from the bustle of our crowded lives can be a renewal of the peace that God gives when we truly desire it. Picture the immense distances, the utter isolation, of the desert above which Moses climbed to speak with God. Stand on Mount Sinai and consider that awesome presence. God comes to Moses in majesty, like a devouring fire which lights but does not destroy.

God comes to us in every moment of our lives, enlightening us with the fiery tongues of the Spirit, strengthening us by the silent power of the Spirit within us. Whenever you pray, begin by knowing that you are in the presence of the all-holy God. Allow yourself to be awed by this presence.

Which command of God is the most difficult for me to follow? More importantly, why?

Thank God for always reaching out in mercy and compassion. Give praise that God is always ready to forgive, whatever may have happened between us.

———

Almighty God, we praise your gracious love that meets us in the deep valley as well as on the high mountain. Grant that we may both rejoice in the marvelous life given in Jesus and answer your call to live as he lived.

**Love God
and keep the
commandments.**

Week 2: Tuesday

Mountain of Acceptance

Deuteronomy 34:1, 4–6

Moses went up from the plains of Moab to Mount Nebo, to the top of Pisgah, which is opposite Jericho, and the LORD showed him the whole land. The LORD said to him, "This is the land which I swore to Abraham, to Isaac, and to Jacob, saying, 'I will give it to your descendants'; I have let you see it with your eyes, but you shall not cross over there." Then Moses, the servant of the LORD, died there in the land of Moab, at the LORD's command. He was buried in a valley in the land of Moab, opposite Bethpeor, but no one knows his burial place to this day.

At the end of the forty years of wandering in the wilderness, the Israelites come to the border of the Promised Land. Moses climbs a mountain as he had done to receive the Law on Mount Sinai. Moses has led the

Chosen People out of Egypt, taught them, admonished and encouraged them, and shared in their privations. In the chapters before this passage, he has given them further instruction about the next stage in their life, blessed them in their tribes, and appointed Joshua as his successor. But now, he only looks upon the Promised Land without entering it. For Moses, it is time to let go and hand the future to others.

We all need to let go when it is time, and not only in old age. There are many times in our lives when we must let someone else continue what we have begun. Moses was granted a vision of the land which the Lord had prepared, and he died confident of a great future for God's people.

———————

Quiet yourself as you begin reflecting. You are climbing a mountain. It is steep, the day is hot and the ground is hard, but you hope that if you can cross this mountain you will find great happiness. You reach the top and look down on the most beautiful land that you have ever seen. You long to descend and come closer to that vision, but you are held back by the realization that God is asking you something else. You throw yourself on the ground, despondent, perhaps resentful that all your exertion has brought so little. Then you realize that this beautiful sight is itself a gift from God. You rise, kneel, and thank God for this precious gift, rejoicing with those who are living in the beautiful valley. Inspired by this moment, you prepare to return, strengthened in faith by the splendid vision.

Is there someone who has received the credit for what I have done? If so, what really fuels the discontent I feel? Can I talk about this with God?

Thank God for something beautiful, great or small, that has enriched your life.

———————

Loving God, guide and protector of all who follow you in faith, grant us a love that rejoices with those who rejoice and does not turn away because of disappointed hope. Open our eyes to see your creating love that has made all, and your caring love that sustains all.

**We are all children
of the Promise.**

Week 2: Wednesday

Mountain of Temptation

Matthew 4:8–11

The devil took Jesus to a very high mountain and showed him all the kingdoms of the world and their splendor; and he said to him, "All these I will give you, if you will fall down and worship me." Jesus said to him, "Away with you, Satan! for it is written, 'Worship the Lord your God, and serve only him.'" Then the devil left him, and suddenly angels came and waited on him.

The final victory over sin and death was won on the Cross, but it is good to remember the importance of those forty days when our Lord confronted evil and refused its false offers. Jesus' first temptation, to assuage his hunger by turning stones into bread, was dismissed because he refused to use his divine power for his own advantage. The temptation in our reading today was something different: to establish God's kingdom without the Cross, without long years of waiting for his time to come, without the sufferings to be faced by generations to come. But the price was unthinkable, that of calling evil good, of making a deliberate choice for power rather than patiently seeking the will of God. Jesus refused to follow the tempter, and chose instead the way that would lead to Calvary.

Be still for a moment as you begin. You are still on the mountain from which you looked into the beautiful valley. You have thanked God for the sight of it and are preparing to descend the way you came. But a new idea occurs to you. If you take another path back down the mountain, surely there would be so much that you could do for God. Your old life seems to be making no progress; you have done what you can, and it is time to move on. Just going down the mountain a different way shouldn't matter…. After all, you cannot stay where you are, and it would be a waste of that strenuous climb just to look at the view and then return to the same old place. God cannot really have intended that, because you want to do the Lord's work as well as find a sense of fulfillment. Then you think of the cross, and remember that being a disciple means following Jesus even when it's the last thing you want.

Am I able to acknowledge the reason why a particular habit of wrongdoing is so hard for me to reject?

Thank God for giving you strength against temptation. Give praise for the example of Jesus, who in his humanity knew what it means to be tempted.

———

Understanding God, in whose Son Jesus
Christ we have both a pattern of obedience and
the power that saves us from sin, grant that we
may resist all that would turn us away from
you, and follow your Son when we are
tempted in this life.

**Worship and serve
the Lord your God.**

Week 2: Thursday

Mountain of Teaching

Matthew 5:1–11

When Jesus saw the crowds, he went up the mountain; and after he sat down, his disciples came to him. Then he began to speak, and taught them, saying:

"Blessed are the poor in spirit, for theirs is the kingdom of heaven.
"Blessed are those who mourn, for they will be comforted.
"Blessed are the meek, for they will inherit the earth.
"Blessed are those who hunger and thirst for righteousness, for they will be filled.
"Blessed are the pure in heart, for they will see God.
"Blessed are the peacemakers, for they will be called children of God.
"Blessed are those who are persecuted for righteousness', for theirs is the kingdom of heaven.

"Blessed are you when people revile you and persecute you and utter all kinds of evil against you falsely on my account."

The "Sermon on the Mount"—of which this is only part—has attracted people of many different faiths. As the previous verses tell us, Jesus had attracted a vast number of people by his healing miracles. Here, he goes up the mountain to get away from the crowd and gathers his disciples, his close followers, around him.

What they hear is far from simple. It is a reversal of selfish values, and a promise of blessing for those whom the world might regard as inadequate or unfortunate. It is not the promise of an easy life; those who follow Jesus may find that their way leads even to persecution.

———————

Quietly imagine yourself on the mountain. You are there, close to Jesus. Perhaps you have become one of his followers. Or, perhaps curious about this new teacher who has performed such wonderful cures, you have climbed the mountain with the others and slipped in quietly among them. What are you expecting to hear? How to cure sick people? How to keep the Law and interpret it in your daily life? How to gain some secret knowledge about finding eternal happiness?

Read the words of the passage again, trying to encounter them as if for the first time. How do they relate to you? Do you want to accept these blessings with all that they mean for living? There is much more of this Scripture passage; find time to read further and reflect upon what you read.

How do I know when I am trying to follow the teaching of Jesus, not for merit or reward, but simply out of love? Am I ready to accept the new responses that are continually asked of me? What might help me to be more open in this regard?

Thank God for the guidance of Scripture. Give praise for the opportunity to pray quietly with the Word.

————

Father in heaven, you have given us the Scriptures, and especially the Gospel, to guide us throughout our lives. Give us also a deep love of your word, and a true desire to live in the way of your commands.

**Blessed are they who hear
the Word of God and obey it.**

Week 2: Friday

Mountain of Glory

Mark 9:2–8

Jesus took with him Peter and James and John, and led them up a high mountain apart, by themselves. And he was transfigured before them, and his clothes became dazzling white, such as no one on earth could bleach them. And there appeared to them Elijah with Moses, who were talking with Jesus. Then Peter said to Jesus, "Rabbi, it is good for us to be here; let us make three dwellings, one for you, one for Moses, and one for Elijah." He did not know what to say, for they were terrified. Then a cloud overshadowed them, and from the cloud there came a voice, "This is my Son, the Beloved; listen to him!" Suddenly when they looked around, they saw no one with them any more, but only Jesus.

Again Jesus goes up onto a mountain. He has shown his humanity on the mountain of temptation, and his authority as a teacher on the mountain where he gathered his disciples around him. Now he goes with only three of his closest friends, the "inner circle" of the Twelve, to a mountain traditionally identified as Mount Tabor where the full glory of his divinity is revealed. The appearance of Moses and Elijah, who had experienced the presence of God on mountains, reminds us of Jesus' own love for the Law and the Prophets.

The three disciples see the glory of God which was revealed to a favored few in Israel. The cloud from which the divine voice is heard appears in similar revelations, as the cloud covered Mount Sinai when Moses received the tablets of the Law. Note the reaction of Peter, always the first to speak and often getting it wrong. He wants to stay on the mountain, but the vision fades and they descend. The next verses tell how Jesus immediately responds to a request for healing and resumes his ministry.

———————

Think of the most wonderful moment in your life, a time when you felt the near presence of God and the assurance of divine love. It might have been during private prayer or public worship, or perhaps it was an experience of beauty in nature, music or painting; or maybe it involved a moment when you realized you were in love.

Enter the experience again. You are on the heights, lifted above ordinary living, and you long to stay there forever. Surely this is what God desires for you? But again you must return to daily life. There is work to do, more of life's journey to be followed.

God is as near to you in the valley as on the summit. The glory that was shown you is still around you, even though you may not see it. You cannot be always on the mountain, but you can continually draw strength from its vision.

How can I be more open to God's revelations to me? How can the times of special grace influence my daily life?

Thank God for the many ways revelations have occurred in your life. Praise and adore the supreme revelation: Jesus Christ, Way, Truth, and Life.

———————

Almighty God, maker and sustainer of all creation, open our eyes to see signs of your glory—moments of worship, all kinds of beauty, caring people—and grant us the patient love that finds glory in daily tasks and simple service.

We have beheld God's glory.

Week 2: Saturday

Mountain of Agony

Luke 22:39–46

Jesus came out and went, as was his custom, to the Mount of Olives; and the disciples followed him. When he reached the place, he said to them, "Pray that you may not come into the time of trial." Then he withdrew from them about a stone's throw, knelt down, and prayed, "Father, if you are willing, remove this cup from me; yet not my will but yours be done." Then an angel from heaven appeared to him and gave him strength. In his anguish he prayed more earnestly, and his sweat became like great drops of blood falling down on the ground. When he got up from prayer, he came to the disciples and found them sleeping because of grief, and said to them, "Why are you sleeping? Get up and pray that you may not come into the time of trial."

The Mount of Olives stands to the east of Jerusalem. Here Jesus often went with his disciples, and from here he had ridden into Jerusalem on the humble back of a donkey. Now he goes to Gethsemane, an olive-grove on its lower slope. After times of temptation, of teaching, and of glory, he has come to Jerusalem. A few days before he had been hailed by an excited crowd. Now he has only his closest followers with him. One has gone to betray him and the others have fallen asleep while he wrestles with the knowledge of what the following day must bring. Temptation returns, the natural human wish to avoid suffering and escape death. But, as in the wilderness, Jesus remains focused on God's will. We ponder the mystery in awe.

Spend a moment in silence before you begin. It is dark, the time of night when one's resistance is at its lowest. You are awake, while all the rest of the world seems to be sleeping. Think of the nighttime terrors, occurring during those hours when all seems lost and trouble overwhelms you. There is no comfort; even those dearest to you are asleep and unknowing.

That is only a tiny fraction of the Lord's suffering in Gethsemane. Nothing exists now but you and God who loves you and brought you to this moment. You call on

God, remember the promise and wait to be brought from darkness into light.

When I become weary, what image of God keeps me going? When it seems impossible to pray, can I just remain quietly in God's gaze?

Thank God for loving you even in the darkest times. Praise Jesus the Savior who knows the experience of human terror.

———————

Good Lord, in all our fear, let us keep before our eyes the picture of your moment of fear, knowing that you are with us even now.

**Not as I will,
but as God wills.**

WEEK 3: LIGHT

Light is perhaps the most powerful, the most funda-
mental and the most widely shared image of God. From
ancients who worshiped the sun to we who are gifted with
the spiritual significance of light in the Gospels, people
have recognized the mystery of light and its opposite, darkness. As we continue our journeys and climb our mountains, we need the light of God to keep us on the right
path. This week we will think of some of the many ways
in which Scripture interprets the meaning of light. We
pray to live our journey in the wonderful light that God
gives us.

Week 3: Monday

Light of Creation

Genesis 1:1–5

In the beginning when God created the heavens and the earth, the earth was a formless void and darkness covered the face of the deep, while a wind from God swept over the face of the waters. Then God said, "Let there be light"; and there was light. And God saw that the light was good; and God separated the light from the darkness. God called the light Day, and the darkness he called Night. And there was evening and there was morning, the first day.

Scripture begins with a declaration of light as the first and basic act of creation. We can only speak in these terms of time, since the ultimate mystery of timelessness is beyond our grasp in this life. Light brings the image of existence rather than nothing, of the difference between being and non-being. All that follows in creation rests upon the division between light and darkness.

The biblical writers continually remember and express this in various ways. The Psalms give us words to declare, "The Lord is my light and my salvation," and to acknowledge our dependence on God, "In your light shall we see light" (Ps 27:1; 26:9). Isaiah writes of God's mercy toward Israel, "The people who walked in darkness have seen a great light; those who lived in a land of deep darkness—on them light has shined" (9:2). The light of God's glory breaks upon the shepherds who first hear of the birth of Jesus (Lk 2:8–9), and St. John describes the coming of Christ as "the true light" (Jn 1:9).

By describing the separation of day and night, the writer of Genesis reminds us of the rhythm which gives a firm framework to our lives. Later, God's promise to Noah reminds us that the rhythm will be maintained and that the seasons, and day and night, will not cease (Gen 8:22). Light continually reveals the glory of creation and reminds us that we are not masters but stewards of what God has made.

———————

Imagine that you are in total darkness. Perhaps it is a sudden power outage or a moonless night in a lonely place.

You have no sense of direction, no knowledge of what is around you. Even what is familiar by day or when the lights are on is no longer under your control. You begin to doubt the boundaries of the world, which a little time ago were unquestioned as the background of your normal experience. Even your own sense of reality seems to be slipping away.

Suddenly light returns to the room or you reach a well-lit road. Confidence surges back and you move freely, soon forgetting the short time of deprivation. You feel more thankful for blessings which you have taken too much for granted. But you also become more aware of the hidden disorder in your life. The light which gives power to move freely is also a call to start tidying up and doing a bit of soul-searching.

How can I let God's light shine more freely in my life so that I can honestly confront my sins? What causes me to avoid reality?

Thank God for the gift of light, for the light of the eye and the light of the soul. Give praise for the love that has given order and pattern to human life.

————

Eternal Light, shine into our hearts.
  Eternal Goodness, deliver us from evil.
  Eternal Power, be our support.

Eternal Wisdom, scatter the darkness
of our ignorance.

The Lord is my light
and my salvation.

Week 3: Tuesday

Light of Guidance

Exodus 13:18, 21; 14:9, 19–20

God led the people by the roundabout way of the wilderness toward the Red Sea. The LORD went in front of them in a pillar of cloud by day, to lead them along the way, and in a pillar of fire by night, to give them light, so that they might travel by day and by night. The Egyptians pursued them, all Pharaoh's horses and chariots, his chariot drivers and his army. The angel of God who was going before the Israelite army moved and went behind them; and the pillar of cloud moved from in front of them and took its place behind them. It came between the army of Egypt and the army of Israel. And so the cloud was there with the darkness, and it lit up the night; one did not come near the other all night.

God led the Israelites out of Egypt and showed them the right way to travel through unknown territory. The sun gives light to the whole world, and the light of God fills our lives if we will open ourselves and let it shine on us. Sometimes, however, we need a special light to show the way through a dark place, and there are times when a new situation or a difficult decision brings us to ask for special grace and guidance.

Scripture continually tells us how individual men and women have been shown the next step in their lives, and often turned back from a way that would have led to disaster. Sometimes it was a clear light, like the pillar of fire which left no doubt of the path to follow. Sometimes it was more like the pillar of cloud, leading step by step but without clear vision or direction. We have all known both of these as God's ways of leading us on, and like the Israelites we have tried to follow in faith. But if we refuse divine guidance and insist on going our own way, life can be dark with our self-will seeming to be a cloud between us and God.

———————

Imagine that you are walking across a big open place in the dark, holding a little pocket flashlight which lights only a very short way in front of you. Suddenly you come within range of a sensor which switches on a powerful floodlight that illuminates the whole area. You see that you have strayed a bit from your path and now it is clear again. But it seems to be a long way compared with a short-cut that could be made from where you now stand, and you set off again in what seems like a more direct route. After a time the floodlight goes out and you are left with your own tiny light, uncertain how to continue and not knowing what obstacles may be in your way. Your only hope is that you will somehow get back into the sensor's range again.

We can take pride in the small lights in our lives: intelligence, money, success, power, having the answers.... But they pale when we step into the light of God's providence and care.

What are my own "flashlights" that I rely on, but which often lead me astray? What inner signals does my heart provide that remind me of God's love?

Thank God for guiding you all through your life, to this day. Give praise for God's loving care that does not leave you to travel alone.

———

Be thou our vision, O Lord of our hearts,
    Be all else as naught to us,
        save that thou art,
    Be thou our best thought by the day
        and the night,

Both waking and sleeping,
thy presence our light.

Ancient Celtic Hymn

The Word of God
is my guiding light.

Week 3: Wednesday

Light of the World

John 1:1–9

In the beginning was the Word, and the Word was with God, and the Word was God. He was in the beginning with God. All things came into being through him, and without him not one thing came into being. What has come into being in him was life, and the life was the light of all people. The light shines in the darkness, and the darkness did not overcome it. There was a man sent from God, whose name was John. He came as a witness to testify to the light, so that all might believe through him. He himself was not the light, but he came to testify to the light. The true light, which enlightens everyone, was coming into the world.

The prologue to the fourth Gospel takes us deep into Christian Revelation, in words that speak to our hearts rather than to our intellectual understanding. Christ not only gives light to the world but is himself that light. Creation and guidance are wonderful, but the living presence of God among us is more wonderful still. He says, "I am the light of the world" (Jn 8:12).

You may have seen the famous picture by Holman Hunt with that title. Jesus stands at a door overgrown with briars—the sins which turn us away from him. He carries a lantern and knocks on the door: the painter combines the theme of light with another saying, "Behold, I stand at the door and knock" (Rev 3:20). The painting conveys a message that is worth our attention. We must turn away from darkness and let the light come in.

Allow yourself a moment of silence. Imagine that you are comfortable in your living room with the door closed, settled in your favorite chair with just enough light for what you are doing—perhaps enjoying a book, listening to music, or relaxing another way. It has been a long and busy day, and you feel entitled to a little time to yourself. Then you hear knocking at the front door, gentle but urgent at the same time. Is it someone you want to see, perhaps a friend? Or is it someone with a need who will take up your leisure time? Eventually you get up and open the door a crack, and a great light begins to enter. It is immeasurably bright, and as you open the door further it floods the room, filling you with a sense of being loved and cherished. Sit and be quiet in the wonder of Christ the Light.

What are my selfish concerns that try to shut out the divine light from my life? When do I most feel cherished by God?

Thank God for being present in your everyday life. Give praise for the coming of Christ, the Light of the World.

———————

Christ, our Savior, keep us from being content with the dimness that is not you, so that we may open the doors of our hearts to your everlasting and saving Light.

**Christ, be my light today
and every day.**

Week 3: Thursday

Light of Choosing

"For God so loved the world that he gave his only Son, so that everyone who believes in him may not perish but may have eternal life. Indeed, God did not send the Son into the world to condemn the world, but in order that the world might be saved through him. Those who believe in him are not condemned; but those who do not believe are condemned already, because they have not believed in the name of the only Son of God. And this is the judgment, that the light has come into the world, and people loved darkness rather than light because their deeds were evil. For all who do evil hate the light and do not come to the light, so that their deeds may not be exposed. But those who do what is true come to the light, so that it may be clearly seen that their deeds have been done in God."

Years ago I overheard a conversation in a French restaurant. A diner asked what on the menu was particularly good, to which the waiter replied in French, "Everything is good, you only have to choose." Unfortunately, life is not usually so simple and not everything that we can choose is good. The human ability to choose is expressed in the story of the Garden of Eden and appears many times in Scripture in the stark alternatives of choosing blessing or curse, light or darkness, life or death.

God has a purpose for each of us and will guide us if we will follow, but we can choose not to follow God's guidance. This passage comes after Jesus meets with Nicodemus, who hears that he must be born again and become new to enter the Kingdom of God. To be born again means to turn to Jesus, who is blessing, light, life. The light which guides us reveals us to ourselves and also reveals the path that leads to life.

———————

Quietly imagine a divided path which offers two possible directions. One is wide and smooth, but so dark that you can see only a little way ahead. The other is brightly lit but it leads steeply upwards and is stony under foot. You take what looks like the easier way, but it soon proves to be full of obstacles and strange shapes which are frightening in the darkness, so you turn back and thankfully follow the way of light.

Think of a time in your life when you chose wrongly, perhaps from misjudgment or perhaps because the decision, although clearly wrong, was attractive. What made you realize you were on the wrong path? Has God brought light into your darkness this Lent?

What recent choice do I regret? Is there something I can do to be more aware of God's guiding light?

Give thanks for the light of Christ that shines through all doubts and perplexities. Praise God who came to be our Savior.

———————

Providing God, who sent the Son into our world, grant that we may turn away from darkness, toward the light shining on the face of Christ.

**Love the truth
and follow the light.**

Week 3: Friday

Light of Change

Acts 26:9, 12–18

I was convinced that I ought to do many things against the name of Jesus of Nazareth. With this in mind I was traveling to Damascus with the authority and commission of the chief priests, when at midday along the road I saw a light from heaven, brighter than the sun, shining around me and my companions. When we had all fallen to the ground, I heard a voice saying to me in the Hebrew language, "Saul, Saul, why are you persecuting me? It hurts you to kick against the goads." I asked, "Who are you, Lord?" The Lord answered, "I am Jesus whom you are persecuting. But get up and stand on your feet; for I have appeared to you for this purpose, to appoint you to serve and testify to the things in which you have seen me and to those in which I will appear to you. I will rescue you from your people and from the Gentiles—to whom I

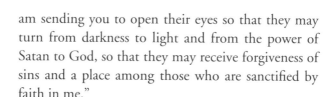

> am sending you to open their eyes so that they may turn from darkness to light and from the power of Satan to God, so that they may receive forgiveness of sins and a place among those who are sanctified by faith in me."

This is St. Paul's own testimony to his conversion of heart. To be a Christian is to know the powerful light of Christ that guides and teaches us. Saul is thrown to the ground by its force, temporarily blinded until he receives new sight and sees the whole world differently. This is the Gospel's call: to leave the old ways and follow the new. Saul the persecutor of the Church was changed on the Damascus Road into its most fervent missionary. Paul continually exhorts us to be true to the revelation that we too have known.

The light of Christ may seem to destroy in order to create, to take away so that something else can be given. Perhaps we do not think we need a Damascus Road; but following Christ means always being open to a new calling and fresh insight.

In silence, imagine that you are in a dim room where the lamplight is not very strong. It is a rather shabby and untidy room, but it is comfortably familiar, and you do not want to make the effort of changing anything or add-

ing more lamps. Suddenly, a bright light fills the room. Everything is still there, still recognizable—and yet different. You are surprised, uncomfortable, a bit resentful at this interference with what has long been familiar. Yet, as you sit with the experience, you begin to feel strangely excited about the new possibilities. You open the door, and again everything outside is the same and yet... different. It takes courage to step out into that clear light, but you feel sure that all will be well.

Am I always open to receive new calls from God? What do I use to distract myself from what God may be asking?

Thank God for the shocks and surprises that have changed your life for the better. Give praise for all who have helped you to know yourself and God more clearly.

———

Dear Lord, guide us back to the right path when we wander away, and open our eyes to see your light of truth.

In your light we shall see light.

Week 3: Saturday

Eternal Light

Revelation 21:22–24; 22:3–5

I saw no temple in the city, for its temple is the Lord God the Almighty and the Lamb. And the city has no need of sun or moon to shine on it, for the glory of God is its light, and its lamp is the Lamb. The nations will walk by its light, and the kings of the earth will bring their glory into it. The throne of God and of the Lamb will be in it, and his servants will worship him; they will see his face, and his name will be on their foreheads. And there will be no more night; they need no light of lamp or sun, for the Lord God will be their light, and they will reign forever and ever.

Scripture begins and ends with light. At the moment of creation God says, "Let there be light." Now, in the vision of heaven which the author of the Book of Revelation tries to express in human language, the marvel of divine light is taken up again and made perfect. The sun and moon were created so that we might have light and know the rhythms of night and day. In God's presence they are no longer needed, for God is light, goodness, mercy and love. We cannot fully understand God's ultimate mystery, but the words of those who have been granted special insight can help us in our contemplation.

Now in the middle of Lent, we continue to adore our glorious God. Thanksgiving, contrition, and intercession are all essential aspects of prayer, along with adoration: praising God who not only gives light to our lives, but who *is* Light.

———

Sit quietly and let the light of God enfold you. Feel the radiance of divine love pouring out through the angels, the saints of all ages, the prayer and work of the Church, and the wonder of creation. Feel it in the love of those who love you and have helped to bring you to this time of adoration. Draw it into the depth of your being and let it shine on all you hold in your heart. Do not try to remember the world's many needs, for they are too many for our minds to grasp. Let everything simply be drawn into the radiance of God, the eternal light. Be still, and let God love you as you are.

As we come to the end of our week of meditating on the light of God, let us find its completion in the words of

Scripture: "It is he alone who has immortality and dwells in unapproachable light, whom no one has ever seen or can see; to him be honor and dominion" (1 Tim 6:16).

How might I recognize the dark areas of my life more readily? Is there someone who might be able to help me see myself more honestly by shining light upon my reality?

Thank God for the promise of eternal life through Jesus Christ. Give praise for the glory that we cannot now comprehend, but that we hope to share after death.

––––––––

Lord Jesus, kindle within us the lamp of your love, so that one day we may live in your perpetual light.

Eternal light, shine on me.

WEEK 4: NOURISHMENT

We do not need to be reminded that food and drink are essential for our lives. We soon become hungry if we have to wait longer than usual before eating. We enjoy meals with friends, and that brings us together in moments of community. All these aspects appear in Scripture: God gives us our daily food and has pity on the hungry; God's people know the pleasures of a feast, and they are happy together as they eat. We thank God for the good things of this world, but we also see them as signs of spiritual grace. Jesus tells his followers to hunger and thirst for righteousness. Through stories of eating and drinking, we find ways to grow nearer to God.

During this week, let us make a special offering of some abstinence in food or drink, as thanksgiving for our own nourishment, and to accompany our intercession for the millions in the world who are continually hungry.

Week 4: Monday

Water of Strife

Exodus 17:1, 3–7

The whole congregation of the Israelites journeyed by stages as the LORD commanded. They camped at Rephidim, but there was no water for the people to drink. But the people thirsted for water; and the people complained against Moses and said, "Why did you bring us out of Egypt, to kill us and our children and livestock with thirst?" So Moses cried out to the LORD, "What shall I do with this people? They are almost ready to stone me." The LORD said to Moses, "Go ahead of the people, and take some of the elders of Israel with you; take in your hand the staff with which you struck the Nile, and go. I will be standing there in front of you on the rock at Horeb. Strike the rock, and water will come out of it, so that the people may drink." Moses did so, in the sight of the elders of Israel. He called the place Massah and Meribah, because the Israelites quarreled and tested the LORD, saying, "Is the LORD among us or not?"

The going was hard. The Israelites had escaped from slavery in Egypt, been brought miraculously across the sea, and been guided on their way by the divine presence in cloud and fire. But soon the desert revealed its menace through lack of water. Parched and weary, they forgot all that Moses had endured and done for them. They even forgot God's merciful protection and broke into angry recriminations. Why had they listened to the promise of redemption? Even the life of a slave was preferable to death by thirst! And once more, in infinite love and patience, God had mercy on them and provided for their physical needs.

The memory of the people's ingratitude remained for centuries in the nation's conscience. They did not forget that day in the wilderness when they had tested God (cf. Ps 95:8), and the miracle of water was remembered as "the water of strife" (Ps 106:32), reminding them of God's exquisite mercy.

————

Try to imagine a terrible thirst, one that millions in the world know daily. You can think of *nothing* except water. The physical yearning takes over and reason vanishes. You rage in your misery; perhaps you blame and accuse God. How vividly you remember drinking something cool, and wish you had valued it more fully. What little gratitude you perhaps felt for such mercies. At last, you stumble forward and reach a spring of fresh water, and soon your thirst is relieved. All is well again and as you resume your life, you resolve never again to take God's gifts for granted.

How do I react when things go wrong? Ask yourself honestly: do the demands of Christian faith make me wish that I was not so committed to following Jesus?

Thank God for all that keeps you healthy and strong. Give praise for God's unending patience and love, always available in times of difficulty.

———

God our Father, who brought water out of the rock so that your people should not perish, give us a thankful heart for the gifts that sustain us in this world and a deep thirst for you, the Giver of all that is good.

God freely gives us the water of life.

Week 4: Tuesday

Food for Service

1 Kings 19:1, 3–8

Ahab told Jezebel all that Elijah had done, and how he had killed all the prophets with the sword. Then [Elijah] was afraid; he got up and fled for his life…. He himself went a day's journey into the wilderness, and came and sat down under a solitary broom tree. He asked that he might die: "It is enough; now, O LORD, take away my life, for I am no better than my ancestors." Then he lay down under the broom tree and fell asleep. Suddenly an angel touched him and said to him, "Get up and eat." He looked, and there at his head was a cake baked on hot stones, and a jar of water. He ate and drank, and lay down again. The angel of the LORD came a second time, touched him, and said, "Get up and eat, otherwise the journey will be too much for you." He got up, and ate and drank; then he went in the strength of that food forty days and forty nights to Horeb the mount of God.

Elijah had had enough. He had fearlessly done the Lord's work, culminating in a spectacular contest with the priests of Baal which had proved the supremacy of the God of Israel. But Jezebel, the wife of King Ahab, had a long-standing feud with Elijah and was after his blood. Elijah was ready to give up, weary of his task, weary of life itself. The divine calling to be a prophet had brought him nothing but toil and danger.

When Elijah was at his lowest ebb, God met both his physical and his spiritual needs — how often these are connected in the stories of Scripture. Food and drink revive the body and also show God's loving care. Elijah received strength for the next stage in his calling, the journey to the sacred Mount Horeb, where God had given water from the rock. There Elijah met the very Spirit of God in a "still, small voice." Then, filled with new spiritual power, he convinced Ahab to repent after yet another fall, and prepared Elisha to be his own successor as a prophet. The whole story is a lesson about perseverance.

———————

Recall a great disappointment you have suffered: work done with no result and no credit, frustrated hope, lack of support by those from whom you expected help. Remember it now in all its bitterness: do not conceal the hurt from yourself. Perhaps you did your best at the time to take it well, not to brood upon it and become resentful.

But was some of the hurt driven inside, repressed and not really healed? Resentment is one of the most destructive emotions. It eats away at the good inside us, and it can be worse when we pretend that it has gone.

Set your memory free to be true to itself, and to recognize also the many times that good has come out of apparent failure. What valuable lessons have you learned, and how often have you taken a different path forward, helped by a strength that was not your own? Now, resolve to let go of any resentment lingering inside you. Eat and drink the spiritual food that God provides.

What kind of difficulty tempts me to give up easily when the Christian way becomes hard? If this Lent seems tedious and discouraging, what may be lacking?

Thank God for all the times you have been brought out of despair into new hope. Give praise for everything that keeps you going in body and soul.

———

Lord God, as you sustained your Chosen People with food and drink in their need, you provide for us a new Bread and new Wine, by which we are brought to eternal life. Grant us a yearning for this Heavenly Food: Yourself, our Master and Lord.

**God will keep me
firm to the end.**

Week 4: Wednesday

Food of Growth

Psalm 23

The LORD is my shepherd, I shall not want.

He makes me lie down in green pastures;
    he leads me beside still waters;

he restores my soul.
    He leads me in right paths for his name's sake.

Even though I walk through the darkest valley,
        I fear no evil;
    For you are with me; your rod and your staff—
        they comfort me.

You prepare a table before me in the presence
        of my enemies;
    you anoint my head with oil; my cup overflows.

Surely goodness and mercy shall follow me
        all the days of my life,

and I shall dwell in the house of the Lord
    my whole life long.

This is perhaps the best known and loved of all the Psalms. Generations of believers have found special comfort in its image of God's loving care. But the psalm is more complex than it may appear. It begins with the familiar idea of God as a shepherd, easily grasped by the pastoral community of Israel, which depended a great deal on its flocks. Isaiah says that God "will lead his flock like a shepherd" (40:11) and Jesus speaks of himself as the Good Shepherd (Jn 10:11–18).

In this psalm we first hear how God will always provide for the Chosen People the food and drink they need, the green pastures and the still waters. God will protect them with the rod or club that drives away wild beasts and with the staff that guides the flock in the right way. Even as they go through a dark valley—or as we often hear it, "the valley of the shadow of death"—they are not afraid because God is with them. Then the psalm offers another thought. The one who prays these words is no longer like a sheep but is an honored guest at a banquet: justified against accusers, fed not with grass and water but with choice food and wine, anointed like a priest or like royalty.

Yesterday we reflected on perseverance in the Christian life; here is a promise not only of continuity but of growth.

We are to mature, to be ready to grow in grace, while still acknowledging our dependence on our Shepherd.

———————

You have been trying to live as a Christian, trusting in God and doing your best. But has it become a routine—praying daily, celebrating the sacraments, doing acts of kindness and charity? Perhaps you are sincere enough, but have your attempts to follow Christ become mere habits?

Imagine that suddenly, something more is offered to you. You receive an invitation to a deeper prayer life, a more complete opportunity to serve. Slowly, you leave the peaceful but familiar green fields where sheep are grazing. You are filled with uncertainty, but then are welcomed into a brightly lit room filled with splendor. You stand amazed as you receive new gifts from the God of love.

How has my Christian life become routine? In what ways do I need to become more adult in my faith?

Thank God for protecting you and leading you to this moment. Ask for whatever nurturing you may need.

———————

Loving Shepherd, guide and protector, lead us in your way, giving us wisdom to discern the richer food of holiness and the grace to desire its strength within.

**Goodness and mercy
will follow me all my life.**

Week 4: Thursday

Hunger of Obedience

Matthew 4:1–4

Then Jesus was led up by the Spirit into the wilderness to be tempted by the devil. He fasted forty days and forty nights, and afterwards he was famished. The tempter came and said to him, "If you are the Son of God, command these stones to become loaves of bread." But he answered, "It is written, 'One does not live by bread alone, but by every word that comes from the mouth of God.'"

A man who had been a prisoner of war in Asia once told me that, among all his privations and sufferings, the thought of food preoccupied him the most. Few of us have experienced extreme hunger—though millions in the world are habitually without enough to eat—but we know how even a temporary lack of food can affect our concentration and our temper. Jesus had fasted for forty days—the length of Lent, during which we try to more closely follow his example. How easily he, the Son of God by whom all things were made, could have satisfied his raging hunger. But our Lord never performed a miracle for his own comfort or advantage: he had set aside his divine power to become fully human, and he refused no discomfort or pain that we experience. Instead, he refused temptation with a scriptural reminder that our souls need the Word of God as much as our bodies need food (cf. Deut 8:3).

You have spent time imagining extreme thirst. Now try to imagine hunger greater than anything you have known. Forty days and nights have passed, burning with heat by day and intensely cold at night, in this desert where you have gone to pray and to meditate on what you are called to do in this world. Could you still value the things of the Spirit before the needs of the body?

Think of those who have suffered extreme hunger and other privations, and yet have kept their faith and even brought it to others. Ask for greater strength to resist the temptation of compromising faith and integrity for present satisfaction.

What might prevent me from allowing myself to feel hungry? Are there other things I might fast from besides food?

Thank God for the grace that allows you to remain focused when you feel rebellious. Pray for those who have too little to eat and for those who are unable to say "no."

Blessed Lord, who suffered the pains of
hunger willingly, give us wisdom to recognize
temptation and the grace to remain centered
on you, the Bread of life.

**I am hungry
for the Word of God.**

Week 4: Friday

Food of Compassion

Mark 6:34–36, 38, 41–44

Jesus saw a great crowd; and he had compassion for them, because they were like sheep without a shepherd; and he began to teach them many things. When it grew late, his disciples came to him and said, "This is a deserted place, and the hour is now very late; send them away so that they may go into the surrounding country and villages and buy something for themselves to eat." He said to them, "How many loaves have you? Go and see." When they had found out, they said, "Five, and two fish." Taking the five loaves and the two fish, he looked up to heaven, and blessed and broke the loaves, and gave them to his disciples to set before the people; and he divided the two fish among them all. And all ate and were filled; and they took up twelve baskets full of the broken pieces and of the fish. Those who had eaten the loaves numbered five thousand men.

This remarkable story is the only one of Jesus' miracles that is described in all four Gospels. Clearly it was an event which the early Christians regarded as important. Jesus performed this miracle out of compassion for hungry people in a difficult situation. Jesus not only refused to use his divine power for his own benefit, he refused to use it simply as a spectacle to demonstrate that power. His miracles were conscious acts of love.

What is more, we read how the meal Jesus provided was not only sufficient for the present, urgent need. There was more food than the hungry crowd could manage, just as there had been a great provision of wine at the marriage in Cana (cf. Jn 2:1–12). God's bounty is unlike anything we know. Further, this action of Jesus prefigures what he did at the Last Supper: he took bread, offered thanks, broke it, and gave it. This is what is done at every Eucharist, and the Gospel writers record it as a sign of the even greater miracle that was to come.

————

Allow yourself a moment of silence as you begin reflecting. It has been an exciting day. You have been one of the crowd following this new teacher and healer of whom everyone has heard so much. The power of his words and the company of others filled with the same enthusiasm have made you forget about eating and about the distance you have walked. Now it is late, the day is colder, and you are a long way from either home or the chance of buying food. The excitement fades; your spirits begin to lag and your body cries out for food. Perhaps you even begin to grumble about religious people who are full of pious words but do nothing to help physical needs.

Meanwhile, those who are close to the Teacher start organizing everyone into groups. This seems to be just one more irritation, but you sit down for want of anything better to do. But then, food is passed around. You find yourself eating, offered more than you can possibly take. And with the food comes a new contentment, a sense of fellowship with strangers who have shared your need and now share your satisfaction. Eventually the crowd disperses. Do you walk away, glad to be finally filled, or do you stay with the one who has shown you such love?

In what ways do I share Jesus' compassion for the needs of others? What are some blessings I have received that others may need?

Thank God for the grace that enables you to understand the needs of others in this world. Praise God's divine love, caring for all our needs.

———————

Lord, whose love never fails and whose
compassion meets us in our weakness and
need, as our bodies are fed from the bounty of

creation, so may we look to feed others in need, so that together we may enjoy your presence among us.

Bread of Heaven, feed me now and evermore.

Week 4: Saturday

Food of Salvation

1 Corinthians 11:23–27

I received from the Lord what I also handed on to you, that the Lord Jesus on the night when he was betrayed took a loaf of bread, and when he had given thanks, he broke it and said, "This is my body that is for you. Do this in remembrance of me." In the same way he took the cup also, after supper, saying, "This cup is the new covenant in my blood. Do this, as often as you drink it, in remembrance of me." For as often as you eat this bread and drink the cup, you proclaim the Lord's death until he comes. Whoever, therefore, eats the bread or drinks the cup of the Lord in an unworthy manner will be answerable for the body and blood of the Lord.

St. Paul's words follow the Gospel story of the Last Supper and link it specifically with the Eucharistic celebration. We recall Jesus' actions in the feeding miracle that we considered yesterday, now performed even more wonderfully on the last night of his earthly life. It is the night of betrayal, the eve of his passion, when Jesus will give his Body and Blood for the salvation of the world, and allow himself to be ever present with us. We have thought much about God giving us food for both body and spirit, but there has never been any gift as wonderful as this. Christians have faithfully followed our Lord's command and example: "Do this in remembrance of me." And he has been faithfully present with us ever since.

———————

One of life's great pleasures is a meal among friends, and especially with those who are deeply loved and trusted. Imagine that you are there in the Upper Room. You are enjoying just such an occasion, but this time there is a subdued feeling of disquiet. The loved one has talked about going away and of betrayal from within the group. The sense of belonging which has been so strong and beautiful is dissolving, and the future is uncertain. Then the one whom you fear you are about to lose breaks bread and passes the cup, as you have seen him do many times before. But this time it is different, more solemn and yet more joyful. You end the meal and go out together into the darkness.

We cannot hope, cannot dare, to share the exact feelings of the disciples on that night. But our prayerful imagination may give us deeper reverence for that night's divine mystery.

How has regular reception of the Eucharist changed the way I live and love? How could I bring what I experience in the Eucharistic celebration into my workplace or relationships?

Thank God for calling you into the communion of believers, known and unknown, living, dead, and yet unborn. Give praise for the Eucharist, which is itself the greatest Thanksgiving.

Bread of Life and Cup of Blessing, let our hunger and thirst for you ever grow. May we come to you in trust, and go forth to act in your name.

**Christ himself
is our heavenly food.**

WEEK 5: HEALING

The quality of our lives depends to some extent on good health. Although many advances have been made in medical treatment, life today still brings problems of illness and injury. In Scripture, healing is seen as one of the gifts of God. The Gospels tell of many healing miracles done by Jesus, and these are often accompanied by words of pardon and salvation. One such word frequently used in the Greek of the New Testament can refer equally to physical or spiritual healing. As we read some of the biblical healing stories, we may reflect on what we can learn from them about our own spiritual health and our response to God's saving power.

Week 5: Monday

Healing in Response to Prayer

2 Kings 20:1–5

In those days Hezekiah became sick and was at the point of death. The prophet Isaiah son of Amoz came to him, and said to him, Thus says the LORD: "Put your house in order, for you shall die; you shall not recover." Then Hezekiah turned his face to the wall and prayed to the LORD: "Remember now, O LORD: I implore you, how I have walked before you in faithfulness with a whole heart, and have done what is good in your sight." Hezekiah wept bitterly. Before Isaiah had gone out of the middle court, the word of the LORD came to him: "Turn back, and say to Hezekiah prince of the people, 'Thus says the LORD, the God of your ancestor David: I have heard your prayer, I have seen your tears; indeed, I will heal you; on the third day you shall go up to the house of the LORD.'"

Hezekiah was faithful in worshiping God. He respected religious duties and wanted peace at a time when his people were threatened by foreign powers. Now he is stricken with an illness so severe that there seems to be no hope of recovery. He does not despair or fall into anger and self-pity, but calls for help to the God in whom he trusts. He makes an act of faith and is restored to the health which he seemed to have lost forever.

Sickness of body or mind, together with other types of distress, is part of our human situation. It is never the desire of our loving Father, who knows how to give his children good things whenever they call upon him. When faced with illness of any kind, we call upon the mercy of our God.

Think of a bad time in your own life: perhaps an illness, depression, anxiety, or a broken relationship. How did you respond? Despite your anger or even despair, were you able to turn to God for guidance and help? How would you respond now? Has this Lent given you new insight into God's presence with us in pain?

How do I bring my grief to prayer? Is there some image of God that gives me comfort in times of sorrow?

Thank God for all the times of healing in your life, whether physical, emotional or spiritual. Give thanks for those who work in the healing ministry, and pray for those who tend the sick of mind or body.

———————

Lord, keep us whole in body, mind, and spirit, faithful when things are bad and thankful when they are good. Give us compassion for the suffering of others and grace to do what works of healing we may.

God's power is made perfect in weakness.

Week 5: Tuesday

Healing of Skepticism

2 Kings 5:1, 9–14

Naaman, commander of the army of the king of Aram...though a mighty warrior, suffered from leprosy. He came with his horses and chariots, and halted at the entrance to Elisha's house. Elisha sent a messenger to him, saying, "Go, wash in the Jordan seven times, and your flesh shall be restored and you shall be clean." But Naaman became angry and went away, saying, "I thought that for me he would surely come out, and stand and call on the name of the LORD his God, and would wave his hand over the spot, and cure the leprosy! Are not Abana and Pharpar, the rivers of Damascus, better than all the waters of Israel?" But his servants approached and said to him, "Father, if the prophet had commanded you to do something difficult, would you not have done it? How much more, when all he said to you was, 'Wash, and be clean'?" So he went down and immersed himself seven times in the Jordan, according to the word of the man of God; his flesh was restored like the flesh of a young boy, and he was clean.

Naaman already feels defensive because of the horrible skin disease that has marred his otherwise successful career. When he comes to see Elisha, he shows also a strong pride in the dignity of his position and contempt for the country he is visiting—human responses which are still all too common today. His servants, less accustomed to special attention, persuade him to do what Elisha tells him, and the healing miracle takes place. Naaman comes to acknowledge and accept the depth that can be found in simplicity.

———

Quietly recall times when you felt your dignity affronted, when you resented the lack of respect or special treatment that you thought was due to you. Think of someone whose advice you ignored because of its simplicity or because you regarded the giver's wisdom as inferior to yours. Perhaps you have thought poorly of a person for being "different" or "foreign," from a country whose customs are different from your own.

Think now of the simplicity of the faith offered in Christ. God works through water, bread, and wine, through familiar language offered in prayer. God's command is that we accept the love that is offered and try to offer it back in our lives.

Is there someone I treat differently (perhaps unconsciously!) because of what he or she believes? What attitudes of mine may reveal that I think my intelligence, my position, or my good works make me a better Christian than others?

Thank God for the way of faith that is open to all, without requiring special gifts. Give praise for the humility of the Incarnation.

———————

Gracious Lord, open our eyes to see the simple signs of hope and to feel the gentle love that is around us through each ordinary day.

**Have faith
like little children.**

Week 5: Wednesday

Healing and Pardon

Mark 2:3–12

Some people came, bringing to Jesus a paralyzed man, carried by four of them. And when they could not bring him to Jesus because of the crowd, they removed the roof above him; and after having dug through it, they let down the mat on which the paralytic lay. When Jesus saw their faith, he said to the paralytic, "Son, your sins are forgiven." Now some of the scribes were sitting there, questioning in their hearts, "Why does this fellow speak in this way? It is blasphemy! Who can forgive sins but God alone?" Jesus said to them, "Why do you raise such questions in your hearts? Which is easier, to say to the paralytic, 'Your sins are forgiven,' or to say, 'Stand up and take your mat and walk'? But so that you may know that the Son of Man has authority on earth to forgive sins"—he said to the paralytic—"I say to you, stand up, take your mat and go to your home." And he stood up, and immediately took the mat and went out before all of them; so that they were all amazed and glorified God, saying, "We have never seen anything like this!"

This is one of the most vivid and exciting stories about Jesus' healing work. His fame has already spread. He is surrounded by people wherever he goes, and will be for the remainder of his life on earth. Except in rare moments when he can withdraw and be alone or rest quietly with his closest followers, there will always be crowds—curious, demanding, praising for a few hours on Palm Sunday, hostile on Good Friday.

It is four friends' persistence that brings the sick man to Jesus, a wonderful account of the power of human affection and the determination to find healing against all odds. They make a hole in the roof; the Greek verb *exorusso*—"to dig out"—is strong, and archaeological excavations in Nazareth have found traces of houses with a layer of earth on a foundation of sticks above the main roof beams. The healing is immediate and complete. The paralyzed man walks away, carrying the bedroll on which he himself had been carried.

There is something more. Before the physical healing, Jesus pronounces forgiveness of sins. As we have seen, illness is by no means the result of sin, and our Lord does not so regard it. But he wants people to be whole in *every* way, spiritually as well as physically.

––––––––––

Quietly imagine being present in the scene on that day in Capernaum. Do you see yourself as sick and in need of healing? As one trying to help a sick friend? As a bystander who takes an objective view? As one who is shocked by the claim to forgive sin? Probably you can relate with all of these positions. Perhaps you have known what it is to be dependent on others, in sickness or in some other difficulty. Perhaps you have felt the love that wants to help the helpless or perhaps you have experienced a great faith event which somehow left you cold or confused. Maybe you have been indignant when a familiar pattern of worship was upset. Resolve to enter more fully into the Gospel stories and relate them to your own life.

Is there someone who may need something from me in order for healing to take place? Is there some area of my life that may need the help of others in order to heal?

Thank God for friendship and human compassion. Give thanks for the love that restores us in body and soul.

––––––––––

Almighty God, grant us constancy in prayer and perseverance in faith. May we so deeply experience a need for you that our sins will be forgiven and our infirmities healed, and we will be made whole.

**Jesus, pardon
and restore me.**

Week 5: Thursday

Healing through Faith

Luke 7:1–10

Jesus entered Capernaum. A centurion there had a slave whom he valued highly, and who was ill and close to death. When he heard about Jesus, he sent some Jewish elders to him, asking him to come and heal his slave. When they came to Jesus, they appealed to him earnestly, saying, "He is worthy of having you do this for him, for he loves our people, and it is he who built our synagogue for us." And Jesus went with them, but when he was not far from the house, the centurion sent friends to say to him, "Lord, do not trouble yourself, for I am not worthy to have you come under my roof; therefore I did not presume to come to you. But only speak the word, and let my servant be healed. For I also am a man set under authority, with soldiers under me; and I say to one, 'Go,' and he goes, and to another, 'Come,' and he comes, and to my slave, 'Do this,' and the slave does it." When Jesus heard this he was amazed at him, and turning to the crowd that followed him, he said, "I tell you, not even in Israel have I found such faith." When those who had been sent returned to the house, they found the slave in good health.

I n Shakespeare's play *King Lear,* the Earl of Kent, disguised and seeking renewed service with the master who has banished him, says to the King, "You have that in your countenance which I would fain call master." To the question, "What's that?" the Earl replies simply, "Authority."

The centurion had learned through long years of service to exercise and obey authority, and in Jesus he recognized an authority more powerful than military discipline. He knew that the simple word of command from Jesus was enough to give healing, as surely as an officer's order would be passed on and put into effect. But he was too humble a man, despite his rank in the army of the occupying power, to expect a personal visit. He asked some of the Jews whom he had befriended to intercede with this new healer whose reputation had reached him.

———————

Consider the centurion, a man accustomed to being instantly obeyed, as he waited to see if his request would be answered. Unlike this centurion who sent influential

Jews to make his request, we need no representatives to plead for us. Come to the Lord, oppressed by the anxieties and problems of the moment but trusting in God's loving power. Today, offer to God something that is troubling you, even if it seems small and trivial, and ask God to take and heal it. Take another step forward toward a stronger faith life.

Is there an area of my life that I have not been able to bring to God? If so, what might be the reason for my hesitation?

Thank God for drawing near to us as we approach in prayer and for entering not only our homes but our hearts.

Gracious Lord, look mercifully on us and accept our faith that so often falters and hesitates, but still trusts that we can be made clean. Let us trust in the assurance of the Gospel that there is pardon for all who truly seek it.

**Lord, I am not worthy:
but only say the word
and I shall be healed.**

Week 5: Friday

Healing of the Hopeless

Luke 8:43–48

There was a woman who had been suffering from hemorrhages for twelve years; and though she had spent all she had on physicians, no one could cure her. She came up behind him and touched the fringe of his clothes, and immediately her hemorrhage stopped. Then Jesus asked, "Who touched me?" When all denied it, Peter said, "Master, the crowds surround you and press in on you." But Jesus said, "Someone has touched me; for I noticed that power had gone out from me." When the woman saw that she could not remain hidden, she came trembling; and falling down before him, she declared in the presence of all the people why she had touched him, and how she had been immediately healed. He said to her, "Daughter, your faith has made you well; go in peace."

This is a strange episode, not because of the miracle, but because of its position in the Gospel text. Matthew, Mark, and Luke all place it within the story of how Jesus raised the daughter of Jairus: as Jesus is going to Jairus' house, this woman touches him. It is unusual for the Scripture narratives to be interrupted by a second narrative in this way, and the whole passage conveys a sense of something very striking, which the witnesses remembered in detail.

Again, a curious crowd is pressing around Jesus. Peter cannot believe that Jesus would be aware of one touch in a jostling throng; some accounts add other disciples' comments, in a tone almost impatient. But Jesus recognizes the touch of faith, and he grants immediate healing and a blessing of peace.

The Lord is the help of the helpless, the hope of those who have lost hope through long suffering, or who despair over their inability to change. He cares for our smaller troubles as well as the great ones. Healing of a chronic complaint might have seemed less important than restoring a child to a bereaved family, but the urgency of death did not cause Jesus to set aside his compassion for another sufferer.

———

Consider the burden of something urgent to you, now or in the past. Perhaps a medical condition is not responding to treatment; perhaps you have worried about work or money; maybe you are experiencing difficulty in a relationship or struggle with a pattern of sin that lies heavy on your conscience. Put yourself in the Gospel story: feel the pressure of the crowd, the electric atmosphere of mingled hope, excitement and incredulity that surrounds this new healer who is going to raise the dead. You are in the middle of it all, longing for his healing touch but feeling unworthy to approach him. Yet desperation forces you forward to touch his garment and fall at his feet. You can likewise approach him now in prayer and sacrament and know his healing and peace. No trouble, no longing, is too small to bring to him. He who sustains all creation cares for every single creature.

> *Is there a chronic spiritual infirmity in my life, perhaps one that is not immediately visible? What is the first step I could take toward this infirmity's healing?*

Thank God, who never turns away from those who seek in faith. Adore the infinite love that responds to our weakness.

Almighty God, ever watching, ever caring, ever pardoning, cleanse us both in body and soul. Strengthen our faith so that we may always walk in the way of peace.

Remain in
the peace of Christ.

Week 5: Saturday

Healing in the Name of Christ

Acts 3:1–8

One day Peter and John were going up to the temple at the hour of prayer, at three o'clock in the afternoon. And a man lame from birth was being carried in. People would lay him daily at the gate of the temple called the Beautiful Gate so that he could ask for alms from those entering the temple. When he saw Peter and John about to go into the temple, he asked them for alms. Peter looked intently at him, as did John, and said, "Look at us." And he fixed his attention on them, expecting to receive something from them. But Peter said, "I have no silver or gold, but what I have I give you; in the name of Jesus Christ of Nazareth, stand up and walk." And he took him by the right hand and raised him up; and immediately his feet and ankles were made strong. Jumping up, he stood and began to walk, and he entered the temple with them, leaping and praising God.

The most striking impression one receives on turning from the Gospels to Acts is the change in the Apostles. Even after the Resurrection the Gospel shows them as still doubtful and frightened, unable to grasp what has happened. On the day of the Ascension they stand helplessly looking up into the sky until they are told to go and wait for God's next command.

After Pentecost, filled with the Holy Spirit, they are transformed. They preach, perform works of mercy and healing, and begin to suffer persecution in the name of Jesus Christ. They speak confidently in Jerusalem, the great city that is not their native place, where their Master had been killed. They show the power of the risen Lord, who is not a dead teacher but the one in whom the power of God is "let loose into the world."

———————

Try to imagine these things happening in your own city or town. A popular preacher, said to have performed some miraculous cures, has recently been condemned and executed for breaking the law. There has been a rumor that he has been seen alive. Now people are announcing this rumor as a fact and are doing in the preacher's name the same kind of healing that he is said to have done.

Reflect upon the strangeness of it all. Would you have listened to this proclamation of good news? Reflect on the power that used very ordinary people who believed in the Good News to continue Jesus' work so that others may believe.

What are some signs of God's power in my own life? How might I become more aware of God's provident care for me?

Thank God for giving strength to those who trust. Give praise for all those who collaborate in bringing the Good News to others.

———

Be with us, Lord, as we prepare to live this solemn time, together with the whole Church. Open our eyes to recognize your redemptive presence in our lives, and grant us a deeper and stronger faith.

They had been with Jesus.

HOLY WEEK

During Holy Week our prayer focuses on the passion of Christ. We think less of ourselves, less even of sorrow for our sins, and try to come closer to our suffering Savior. Each of the images of our lives which we have been considering in the past weeks has its place in the final story, and we use them as we follow Christ and stand at the foot of his Cross. Some of the many reflections and prayers that have been inspired by the passion may help our meditation.

Holy Week: Monday

Journey to Death

Luke 23:26–32

As they led him away, they seized a man, Simon of Cyrene, who was coming from the country, and they laid the cross on him, and made him carry it behind Jesus. A great number of the people followed him, and among them were women who were beating their breasts and wailing for him. But Jesus turned to them and said, "Daughters of Jerusalem, do not weep for me, but weep for yourselves and for your children. For the days are surely coming when they will say, 'Blessed are the barren, and the wombs that never bore, and the breasts that never nursed.' Then they will begin to say to the mountains, 'Fall on us'; and to the hills, 'Cover us.' For if they do this when the wood is green, what will happen when it is dry?" Two others also, who were criminals, were led away to be put to death with him.

There had been many journeys taken at the command of God since Abram left Ur, and since the children of Israel left Egypt. Jesus and his disciples had journeyed, too, walking a long way during the years of his ministry. There had been rough roads, dark roads, lonely and weary ways, until a road led them from Galilee to Jerusalem for the Passover celebration. The last journey of all was short in human measurement, from the Roman headquarters to a hill on the outskirts of the city, but it was the most significant journey that human feet have ever walked. We cannot fully sense, even in loving imagination, the Lord's suffering on the sorrowful way. The night of betrayal, desertion, and denial had ended in cruel mocking, scourging, and a sentence of death for the Lord of life.

Others were drawn into that moment of suffering humanity. The drama of redemption needed its supporting cast to be complete. Privileged to share the burden, Simon of Cyrene, pressed into service by the hated occupying power, traditionally became one of the first Christian believers. Two criminals walked with Jesus, the sinless one numbered with sinners and suffering with them. Women wept at the pitiful sight, drawing even then on his compassion for the troubles that were to come upon Jerusalem in the next generation.

As I try this week to walk with my Lord,
    May I remember Simon and be willing to bear
        another's burden;
    May I feel true sorrow for the suffering of
        innocence, on that day and still today.
    May I have grace to follow the Way of
        the Cross.

————————

Thanks be to our Lord Jesus Christ,
    For everything you have given us.
O most merciful Redeemer,
    Friend and Brother,
May we know you more clearly,
Love you more dearly,
And follow you more nearly.
                      St. Richard of Chichester

**Take up your cross
and follow Christ.**

Holy Week: Tuesday

Mountain of Suffering

Mark 15:22–27

They brought Jesus to the place called Golgotha (which means the place of a skull). And they offered him wine mixed with myrrh; but he did not take it. And they crucified him, and divided his clothes among them, casting lots to decide what each should take. It was nine o'clock in the morning when they crucified him. The inscription of the charge against him read, "The King of the Jews." And with him they crucified two bandits, one on his right and one on his left.

M any of the mountain events in Scripture have brought people closer to God. Climbing above the level of daily life can give a stronger sense of God's presence, revealed in the solitude of the heights. Now, in a place near Jerusalem, it seems as if God's protecting love has withdrawn itself. The sign of God's glory is hidden in a dying man. On a mountain Jesus met and conquered temptation, showing how humanity could resist evil. On a mountain he went apart to teach his disciples because his popularity had drawn crowds around him. On a mountain his divinity was revealed to a few chosen ones. Now it all seems to have been a failure. He who was declared Son of God in that moment of transfiguration is now naked, helpless, slowly dying on a mountain.

It is not a very great mountain. It is a hill known as "skull place," perhaps because of its shape or perhaps because it was a common site for executions. The familiar name "Calvary" is the Latin equivalent of the Hebrew name. The exact site has been disputed but legends grew up around it, particularly that it was the place where Adam was buried. The association has not a literal but a spiritual message. Here the Second Adam brings to a climax all the wrong that has come from refusing to follow God. The ultimate insult to God becomes the way of salvation.

––––––––––

We can never match the love that is incomparable:
We do not know its fullness until
we are made empty.

There is no place to stand now
     but the place of torment
where a naked hill beckons to the last encounter.

———————

Lord Jesus Christ, raised on a cross upon a hill, lift up our hearts and accept our love in response to your immeasurable love given there.

I glory in the Cross of Christ alone.

Holy Week: Wednesday

Light Departed

Mark 15:33–34

When it was noon, darkness came over the whole land until three in the afternoon. At three o'clock Jesus cried out with a loud voice, "Eloi, Eloi, lema sabachthani?" which means, "My God, my God, why have you forsaken me?"

Darkness falls over the land, as the incarnate Light of the world loses strength. The whole of creation seems to be falling apart, returning to the primal chaos which existed before God said, "Let there be light." It is the darkness that covered Egypt in days past, the darkness in which the blind grope and wander, the darkness in which the betrayer departs from the table of communion. Simeon saw in the infant Jesus the sign of a light to enlighten the Gentiles. Now the ruthless power of a Gentile empire is extinguishing that light. Simeon also prophesied that a sword would pierce Mary's soul. Now she stands by the Cross as her Child perishes and the humanity which began in her leaves the world. The people that walked in light have seen a great darkness.

How can we respond to the horror of that noon of midnight? We are helpless in the dark, even though we can move and feel. Our Lord the uncreated is now more helpless than any creature. Everything has departed. He has no friends but two or three who are faithful yet desolate. He is deprived of clothes, of movement, and is fast losing the power of breath. What can we offer in the darkness but our doubts, our uncertainties, our weakness? There is no response but the love that feebly desires to respond to that breaking heart of divine love.

———————

O come, all, and let us sing unto him
    who was crucified for our sake;
    for seeing him upon the tree Mary spake:
    though thou sufferest crucifixion, yet art thou
    my son and my God.

Ancient prayer for Holy Week

———————

Lord, as we cry out of our own place
    of darkness, hear and forgive.
    Lord, as we cry out in tongues that cannot

speak as they desire, hear and forgive.
Lord, as we cry out in the love that cannot
match the divine Love, hear and forgive.
Lord, lighten my darkness.

Lord—my light
and salvation!

Holy Thursday

Divine Thirst

John 19:28–29

After this, when Jesus knew that all was now finished, he said (in order to fulfill the scripture), "I am thirsty." A jar full of sour wine was standing there. So they put a sponge full of the wine on a branch of hyssop and held it to his mouth.

The Son of God has known human weariness, hunger, disappointment, pain. Now, as his human life ebbs, he feels the extremity of thirst. It has been many hours since he could drink, hours of mocking, scourging, the slow climb under the burden of the cross, and above all the bleeding from brow and back, hands and feet. The divine power that gave water to the people in the wilderness does not intervene now to bring even a single drop of water. Only one of the guards, with rough kindness, offers a sop of the sour wine that was the soldiers' ration.

The evangelist reminds us of the words of the Psalmist, "For my thirst they gave me vinegar to drink" (Ps 69:21).

The physical suffering is extreme. But Jesus' thirst refers to more than bodily need. Scripture often mentions thirst as an image of human desire for God:

> As a deer longs for flowing streams,
> so my soul longs for you, O God.
> My soul thirsts for God,
> for the living God (Ps 42:1–2).

Jesus has promised living water, the water of life, to those who will love and follow him (cf. Jn 4:10; 7:38). Does he now feel the withdrawal of God, suggested in his cry from Psalm 22, "My God, my God, why have you forsaken me"? Does he cry out not only in the flesh but in the desire to be again assured of divinity? Can God be forsaken by God?

On this day, we celebrate the gift of the Eucharist at the Last Supper. The wine that quenches thirst, the wine of human fellowship, becomes also the means of divine presence. The wine that in the evening is declared to be the Blood of Christ finds its fulfillment in the blood of his dying. His wounds complete the promise, assure us that the wine we offer will forever be our communion with him.

———

Run to the fountains for water,
 run swiftly, I say,
 be quick of foot like a hart.
 But who is this fountain?
 God.
 God it is that must and can cool the thirst of
 your soul.
 God it is that will refresh you.

St. Augustine

———————

Lord Jesus, revealing true humanity in bodily need and true divinity through infinite love, may we always thirst for holiness in this world, and by grace drink the water that rises up to eternal life.

I thirst for
the water of life.

Good Friday

The Final Healing

John 19:30
When he had received the wine, he said, "It is finished." Then he bowed his head and gave up his spirit.

I t is finished. The human life that began in Bethlehem
has run its course. But these last words of Jesus on the
Cross do not convey finality, a full stop that marks the
end of a phase in history. The sense of the Greek word in
the Gospel is rather, "It is accomplished"—"It has been
achieved"—the statement of something done and yet continuing in its effect. Our Lord has accomplished the greatest of his healing miracles. Until the end of the world for
all who turn to him in faith, there will be spiritual light
for those who walk in darkness; confident steps for those
who have been limping their way through life; freedom
for those paralyzed by fear and anxiety; cleansing for those

entrapped by sin. It is a cry not of defeat but of ultimate victory.

Yet even while we know the triumph of life over death, on this day we are right to contemplate the terrible price of that victory. Immeasurable love has suffered to bring us salvation. There have been so many deaths before and after this death on Calvary. Many, like Jesus, have died young, struck down when life seemed to be approaching fulfillment. Many, like Jesus, have died innocent, victims of power abused and hostility turned to hatred. Many, like Jesus, have died in great pain, tormented by violence or long illness. But none has died like Jesus, drawing the whole world into the love of his outstretched arms.

––––––––

In the Cross,
    and him who hung upon it,
    all things meet,
    all things need it.
    It is their center and their interpretation.
    For he was lifted up upon it,
    that he might draw everyone
    and all things unto him.

John Henry Newman

––––––––

Lord Jesus Christ, may our contemplation of your great act of love for us inspire us to return love for love. May we recognize your suffering face in those we meet along the way, and try to alleviate thirst, as we would do for you.

**Christ died
that I might live.**

Holy Saturday

Day of Repose

John 19:38–42

Joseph of Arimathea, who was a disciple of Jesus, though a secret one because of his fear of the Jews, asked Pilate to let him take away the body of Jesus. Pilate gave him permission; so he came and removed his body. Nicodemus, who had at first come to Jesus by night, also came, bringing a mixture of myrrh and aloes, weighing about a hundred pounds. They took the body of Jesus and wrapped it with the spices in linen cloths, according to the burial custom of the Jews. Now there was a garden in the place where he was crucified, and in the garden there was a new tomb in which no one had ever been laid. And so, because it was the Jewish day of Preparation, and the tomb was nearby, they laid Jesus there.

It is finished. The sacred body that began human life in a manger is laid in a hastily borrowed tomb. The myrrh brought by the Magi is the only gift that is needed, now that the gold of kingship and the incense of priesthood seem to have been taken away. Friends, who feared to acknowledge Jesus as Lord while he lived, now tend him in death. The struggle is over. Vengeance for the disquieting of established lives has been taken; the menace to authority has been destroyed. There is no threat in a dead body.

Between the agony and the triumph, there is rest. On this day the Church rests and waits. We share the seventh day, the day of God's rest from creation, before the first day of creation newly created. Today there is neither the psalm of dereliction nor the hymn of triumph, only the silence of repose and waiting.

We have tried to share with the disciples and friends of Jesus, and especially with his Mother, the reality of the Paschal Mystery. We have tried to stand at the foot of the cross and open our hearts to his pain. Today we cannot truly feel with the disciples, because we know the end of the story. They are desolate, prevented by the sabbath from giving the last service to the body of their beloved Master. They are restless, torn by despair and forced inactivity. We, instead, can rest after the emotion of the last few days, and in expectation of tomorrow.

———————

Rest today. Be quiet and contented. Thank God for the gift of Lent, its challenges and its opportunities. Feel no pride in anything you have done, no guilt in anything you have failed to do. You have opened yourself to hear God's Word and do God's will, and it is enough. God accepts you as you are, in mercy and love.

Lord, calm the waves of this heart,
    calm its tempests.
    Calm yourself, O my soul,
    so that the divine can act in thee.
    Calm yourself, O my soul,
    so that God is able to repose in thee,
    so that his peace may cover thee.
    Yes, Father in heaven,
    often have we found that the world
        cannot give us peace.
    O but make us feel that you art able
        to give peace;
    let us know the truth of your promise
    that the whole world may not be able
        to take away your peace.

Søren Kierkegaard

————

Gracious God, our guide and our strength
in the days of this Lent, grant that the love of

the Risen Christ may confirm all that has been
achieved, pardon what has been left undone,
and bring us day by day nearer to the eternal
life promised to all who trust in him.

Christ has died.
Christ is risen.
Christ will come again.

BOOKS & MEDIA

The Daughters of St. Paul operate book and media centers at the following addresses. Visit, call or write the one nearest you today, or find us on the World Wide Web, www.pauline.org

CALIFORNIA
3908 Sepulveda Blvd, Culver City, CA 90230 (310) 397-8676
5945 Balboa Avenue, San Diego, CA 92111 858-565-9181
46 Geary Street, San Francisco, CA 94108 (415) 781-5180

FLORIDA
145 S.W. 107th Avenue, Miami, FL 33174 (305) 559-6715

HAWAII
1143 Bishop Street, Honolulu, HI 96813 (808) 521-2731
Neighbor Islands call: 800-259-8463

ILLINOIS
172 North Michigan Avenue, Chicago, IL 60601 (312) 346-4228

LOUISIANA
4403 Veterans Memorial Blvd, Metairie, LA 70006 (504) 887-7631

MASSACHUSETTS
Rte. 1, 885 Providence Hwy, Dedham, MA 02026 (781) 326-5385

MISSOURI
9804 Watson Road, St. Louis, MO 63126 (314) 965-3512

NEW JERSEY
561 U.S. Route 1, Wick Plaza, Edison, NJ 08817 (732) 572-1200

NEW YORK
150 East 52nd Street, New York, NY 10022 (212) 754-1110
78 Fort Place, Staten Island, NY 10301 (718) 447-5071

OHIO
2105 Ontario Street, Cleveland, OH 44115 (216) 621-9427

PENNSYLVANIA
9171-A Roosevelt Blvd, Philadelphia, PA 19114 (215) 676-9494

SOUTH CAROLINA
243 King Street, Charleston, SC 29401 (843) 577-0175

TENNESSEE
4811 Poplar Avenue, Memphis, TN 38117 (901) 761-2987

TEXAS
114 Main Plaza, San Antonio, TX 78205 (210) 224-8101

VIRGINIA
1025 King Street, Alexandria, VA 22314 (703) 549-3806

CANADA
3022 Dufferin Street, Toronto, Ontario, Canada M6B 3T5 (416) 781-9131
1155 Yonge Street, Toronto, Ontario, Canada M4T 1W2 (416) 934-3440

¡También somos su fuente para libros, videos y música en español!